Everything You Need to Know About

The Dangers of Overachieving

A Guide for Relieving Pressure and Anxiety

The drive to achieve perfection can make you successful, but you can also push yourself too far.

Everything
You Need to
Know About

The
Dangers of
Overachieving
A Guide for Relieving
Pressure and Anxiety

John Giacobello

The Rosen Publishing Group, Inc.
New York

Published in 2000 by The Rosen Publishing Group, Inc.
29 East 21st Street, New York, NY 10010

First Edition

Library of Congress Cataloging-in-Publication Data

Giacobello, John
    Everything you need to know about the dangers of overachieving : a guide for relieving pressure and anxiety / John Giacobello.
        p. cm. — (The need to know library)
    Includes bibliographical references and index.
    Summary: A guide for overachievers who wish to relieve anxiety and the pressures of excessive stress, especially when overachieving is becoming a dangerous habit.
    ISBN 0-8239-3107-2 (lib. bdg.)
    1. Overachievement   Juvenile literature. 2. Overachievement—Case studies   Juvenile literature. 3. Stress management   Juvenile literature. [1. Overachievement. 2. Stress (Psychology) 3. Stress management.] I. Title. II. Series.

BF637.O94 G53 2000
155.9'2—dc21   99-045580

Manufactured in the United States of America

Contents

Introduction

Although stress is a normal part of almost everyone's life, we can do things to help ourselves reduce stress or at least learn how to deal with it effectively. This book is about dealing with stress that comes from the pressure to overachieve.

This type of pressure occurs when we feel the need to accomplish more than is humanly possible. It is the pressure to be perfect and to never make a mistake. It is the pressure to prove that we are worthwhile by constantly pushing ourselves beyond our limitations to the point of pain and injury.

This pressure comes from many different sources, both external and internal. It may come from parents, coaches, brothers or sisters, images in the media, and our friends. Often it comes from negative beliefs we hold about ourselves. When we do not like ourselves, achievement might seem to be the only way to show that we have something to offer the world. It makes us feel special, just for that moment. But we may feel that we have to keep achieving more and more to fill the emptiness inside. This kind of thinking can be dangerous to our health; although it is fine to be ambitious and work hard, there is a point when an obsession with overachieving can be damaging. When we lose the ability to realize that we are pushing ourselves too hard, it is time to stop and reevaluate our situation.

Self-esteem, the good feelings or sense of self-worth that we have about ourselves, can also come from somewhere other than our accomplishments. If we love ourselves and believe in ourselves all the time, then overachieving to the point of dangerous habits or behavior (such as not eating properly or not sleeping enough) is not necessary. We need to learn how to pursue (to go after) our goals sensibly and for the right reasons. This book will help you understand the pressure to overachieve and the stress that can result from it. We will suggest ways to deal with this type of anxiety and pressure in order to be able to move toward a healthy way of reaching your goals and making your dreams become a reality.

Overachieving to the point of dangerous habits or behavior, such as not eating properly or not sleeping enough, is not necessary.

Chapter One

Achieving or Overachieving?

*E*verybody admired Amber. She was only in the seventh grade, and her list of accomplishments was already astonishing. Amber was in charge of several school clubs, including the yearbook committee, the science club, and the debate team. She was a straight A student, and she also played on the school's basketball and volleyball teams. The other kids at school thought that there was nothing Amber could not do well.

The strange thing was that she never seemed very proud of her achievements. Amber was always complaining that she should not have missed that one question on the test, that she should have made that one basket she missed, or that it was her fault the debate team lost that one *tournament. She rarely went out with friends or dated. Amber worried that her reputation for being successful intimidated the other students, especially boys, so she avoided socializing.*

Then one day, after performing thirty push-ups using only one hand, Amber collapsed in a heap on the gymnasium floor. Everyone at school was talking about the incident. It was unbelievable that someone as energetic and successful as Amber could ever get sick. Amber's younger sister, Tracey, came to school alone the next day.

"The doctor said that Amber has been driving herself too hard and that she tries to juggle too many activities at once," Tracey explained. "She needs a rest." The kids at school were stunned. Later that evening, Tracey overheard her father talking furiously on the telephone with a school counselor.

"OVERACHIEVER?" he shouted. "My little girl works hard, just like her father! Amber's fine, she just need a day off. Then she'll be ready to get back in the game! You'll see." He slammed down the telephone in a rage.

Amber came downstairs to see what all the fuss was about. Her father threw her a basketball. "You feeling better, hon? Ready for some one-on-one?" Amber looked pale. "I think I'll just go study for a while," she said weakly. Her father

Overachievers believe they constantly have to prove their skills and talents to others by playing sports, studying, playing music, or succeeding in other activities.

beamed. "Sure, go study. You have a lot of schoolwork to make up after laying around here all day."

Overachieving is a term you may have heard used before by teachers, by counselors, by parents, or on television. Some young people are often described as overachievers. But how is overachieving actually defined?

There is no simple definition for this term. An overachiever is not a concrete object, like a toaster. If you take the word "overachieve" apart, you get "over" and "achieve." "Over" in this sense means "too much." And "achieve" means "accomplish" or "perform successfully." Accomplishing is a good thing, and we all want to work as hard as we can to reach our goals. So how can anyone possibly accomplish too much?

Think about great artists who work day and night to create magnificent works of art. What about hard-working Olympic athletes who give 100 percent of their effort in a dramatic struggle for a gold medal. Imagine your favorite music stars, performing long and grueling concerts night after night to keep their fans happy and excited about their songs. Are all of these people overachievers? Do they work too hard and give more than they should?

Actually, overachieving is not correctly defined by how much a person accomplishes, but for what reasons. An overachiever may not necessarily succeed simply because he or she wants to create, win, or succeed. He or she may be doing it for more complicated reasons.

Overcompensating

Sometimes when young people feel badly about themselves, they may feel an urge to overcompensate through achievement. This means that they believe they constantly have to prove their skills and talents to others by playing sports, studying, playing music, or succeeding in other activities. Excelling is the only way they can feel good about who they are. Since they do not love or accept themselves for who they are, they look for external proof (certain facts or things that are visible to others, such as good grades, a nice car, or a certain talent) to show their worth. These people feel tremendous pressure to achieve, which creates stress in their lives.

Jeff was a high school student who always felt uncomfortable with the way his face looked. He disliked the patches of acne that had been popping up since he turned fifteen. And he hated his big nose. He was certain that his nose was the biggest in his whole school. Jeff believed that if he could make his muscles huge and impressive, nobody would notice his face and he might actually find the courage to ask a girl out on a date.

Jeff started working out at the gym every day. After two weeks he was not satisfied with the progress he had made. He wanted to be much more muscular, so he began spending every spare moment he had lifting weights. He ached and sometimes felt serious pain while working out, but he just kept telling himself, "No pain, no gain." Soon he was neglecting homework assignments to go to the gym. His grades began to suffer, and he still did not believe his body was developing the way it should.

Jeff would never be able to satisfy the unrealistic expectations he had of himself. Instead of focusing on his good qualities, he obsessed over what he saw as flaws in his appearance. Working out beyond his capacity was his way of compensating for things he disliked about his looks.

Besides working out for the wrong reasons, Jeff tried accomplishing more than he was really capable of. It was not that he was too weak or lazy to reach his goals, he just expected to be able to achieve more than was humanly possible. He risked serious injury to his body and gambled with his future by slacking off on schoolwork.

How Much Is Too Much?

Sometimes it is difficult to be aware of the fine line between working to our potential and overdoing it. Are we not constantly encouraged to "shoot for the stars"? All the world is inspired by a man or woman who beats the odds and achieves the impossible.

We simply have to develop a sense of our own boundaries. These boundaries are different for everybody, so there is no way somebody else can define them for you. A friend or family member may notice when · you have bitten off more than you can chew, but ultimately you need to be able to see it for yourself.

Bodybuilders and athletes sometimes talk about "good pain" and "bad pain." Good pain refers to the pain and strain of pushing yourself to your limits. It is the feeling you get when you know you are doing all you can to reach your goals. But when you reach your limits and try to move too far beyond them, or move too

When you reach your limits and try to move too far beyond them, it can result in bad pain.

quickly, it can result in bad pain. You know bad pain when you feel it.

When bodybuilders try to lift more weight than they should, they may feel a sharp, shooting pain instead of the usual throbbing pump. Runners who go another three miles after that extra mile might begin to experience shooting pain in their knees. Bad pain can be a sign of injury, and those who try to ignore it may be putting their lives in danger. Fatigue, exhaustion, and difficulty in sleeping can be signs of bad pain from pushing yourself too hard. These are common symptoms of stress.

Types of Overachieving

There are many areas in which young people with self-esteem problems may be tempted to overachieve. In

Fatigue, exhaustion, and difficulty in sleeping can be signs of pushing yourself too hard.

Amber's story, we touched on academics, athletics, and extracurricular activities. These are avenues of achievement that are easily accessible to most students. The pressure to succeed in school and school-related activities can be tremendous, and that pressure can drive some teens to work beyond the boundaries of common sense in order to achieve perfection.

Jeff's chosen area of achievement was his appearance. The teen years are a difficult time, and very few young people are happy with the way their bodies look. This insecurity comes from confusion over physical and hormonal changes that take place during puberty. Most teens will make an effort to look their best, paying careful attention to grooming, personal style, diet, and exercise. But some go too far and put their health at risk by seeking an unattainable ideal.

Some people love to do things to help other people, and that is a wonderful quality. But it can become a problem when generous and helpful people allow their own needs to be neglected. They may spend so much time doing favors for friends, taking care of their family, helping out at school and at work, and volunteering for charity that they have no time left to take care of themselves. Running yourself ragged for others can be a way of overachieving.

We will discuss these and other ways of overachieving throughout this book. Whichever way a young person chooses to overachieve—whether it is by excessive dieting, exercising too much, or running too many miles—it is usually an indication of the same underlying negative feelings. It can also be a sign of difficulty in dealing with pressure, which is a normal part of adolescence.

Chapter Two

Under Pressure

Most young people who attempt to achieve beyond reasonable boundaries are responding to some kind of pressure. The pressure to overachieve can come from many sources, including parents, friends, and coaches. These are called external pressures because they come from forces outside of us. But sometimes the most powerful pressures come from within ourselves and are driven by our thoughts and feelings. Those pressures are called internal. In this chapter we will discuss some sources of pressure to overachieve and how we find both negative and positive ways to deal with them.

External Pressures

Valencia was her stage name, but her real name was Sheesa. She had been a local celebrity, well-known in her hometown of Smallton, Missouri, for her singing and dancing ability. Sheesa performed regularly at dances and other events. Singing made her happier than anything in the world, and she appreciated her Smallton following. But she dreamed of stardom.

Sheesa was determined to make it big. She imagined seeing her name Valencia sparkling in lights on Broadway or rolling across television screens around the world. Her boyfriend, Tommi, was not very supportive of her dreams. He told her that she was foolish and that she would never be talented enough to be truly successful. Many years went by and her big break still did not arrive, so Sheesa began to believe the negative things that Tommi always told her about herself.

Eventually she decided it was time to give up on singing. Sheesa felt that since she was not good enough to make it as a singer, she might as well settle down and raise a family. She married Tommi, not because she wanted to, but because she felt defeated by the music industry. She stopped believing in herself and said good-bye to Valencia for good.

One year later, Sheesa gave birth to a daughter and named her Viva. Viva inherited her mother's beautiful singing voice. Sheesa was thrilled and took

Viva to singing lessons when she was five years old. By age seven, Viva was appearing in television commercials and participating in children's beauty pageants, singing contests, and plays—all arranged by her mother. Viva enjoyed the attention but sometimes wished she could just play with her friends.

As she grew into her teens, the pressure Viva felt from her mother became overwhelming. She had to perform constantly because Sheesa kept arranging concerts for her. She also had to get good grades at school. Dating was out of the question. Although she enjoyed singing, Viva wished she could do it a bit less often. But she did not want to disappoint her mother.

Viva sang beautifully, but sometimes she hit a wrong note or forgot words to the song she was singing, especially when she was feeling tired. Her mother never let those small incidents slide. The audiences did not seem to mind an occasional mistake, but Sheesa did. "You don't make it to the big time by messing up the songs!" she told Viva and grounded her one week for each song not performed perfectly.

Sheesa told her daughter every day that fame and fortune were just around the corner. She had Viva's entire career mapped out, and Viva could not seem to find the courage to tell her she did not want to sing for a living. So she kept on performing and swallowed her objections. Viva felt as though her life was not her own, and never would be.

Pressure from Parents

Our parents are often a source of external pressure. All parents hold some expectations of their children. Many parental expectations are reasonable. Setting rules about doing a fair share of chores around the house is an example of a reasonable parental expectation. But expecting one child to do all of the housework would be considered unreasonable by most people. All parents have differing ideas about reasonable and unreasonable expectations for their own children.

Sometimes parents expect their children to be perfect. Expecting perfection from any human being is unreasonable because no one is perfect. This expectation can create a great deal of stress, especially for a young person who is not fully aware of his or her own boundaries yet. Parents may teach their kids that anyone who makes a mistake is a failure. Sometimes that belief stays with the kids throughout their lives. They may avoid trying anything new because they are afraid of failing.

On the other hand, some of these kids may become overachievers—people who drive themselves too hard and who try to be the best at everything they do. To these kids, achieving may seem like the only way to receive love and approval from their parents.

Some parents (like Viva's mom, Sheesa) may feel

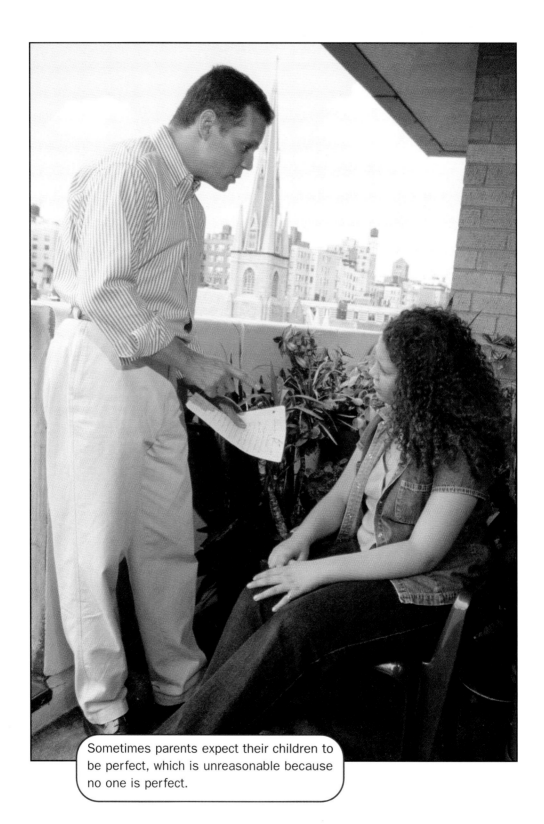

Sometimes parents expect their children to be perfect, which is unreasonable because no one is perfect.

unfulfilled because they never realized their own dreams. They may have wanted to be a singer, a gymnast, or a doctor but were unable to do so for a variety of reasons. Perhaps caring for a child proved to take up more time and energy than they had realized. Or maybe they suffered from low self-esteem and did not believe in themselves enough to see their dreams through. Perhaps they, too, were striving for perfection.

Whatever the case, many parents push their children to achieve what they failed to achieve. They see their children as younger versions of themselves. Pushing their kids into the career they never had or the role they never played is the next most fulfilling thing after not being able to achieve something themselves.

This is not fair to their kids. Everybody has the right to pursue his or her own path in life and travel it at their own pace. Pressure to overachieve that comes from parents is extremely difficult to resist. It can take a long time to find the courage to stand up to one's mother or father when faced with unreasonable expectations. And this pressure may also come from other adult role models, such as a coach, teacher, family friend, or other relative.

Pressure from Your Brother, Sister, or Friends

Jeremy had always loved basketball. He was one of the best players on his school's team, and he worked very hard to keep up his nearly perfect record.

Jeremy's brother, Ralphie, was one year younger than Jeremy. He was not a fan of any sport. Ralphie enjoyed drawing and listening to music more than anything else. His sketches were always praised by his art teacher. But it seemed as if their friends were always comparing Ralphie to Jeremy. They asked them how a big basketball star like Jeremy could have such a wimp for a younger brother. And Jeremy made fun of Ralphie for drawing, teasing him for his lack of athletic ability.

Ralphie became so tired of being treated this way that he decided to learn to play basketball. He spent every spare moment on the court. But no matter how hard he tried, there was just no beating Jeremy. Ralphie's efforts pushed Jeremy to improve his own playing, since he could never face the humiliation of being beaten by his little brother. The two brothers had to outdo one another in every area of their lives, from sports to jobs to who they dated. And Ralphie threw out his charcoal and sketch pad.

Competition between siblings is very common. Just as there is good pain and bad pain, there is also healthy and unhealthy competition. When competition is healthy, those involved understand that they are competing for a positive outcome. They want to help each other become more skilled at what they do.

Jeremy and Ralphie were involved in unhealthy competition. Ralphie gave up doing the things he truly enjoyed because he felt inferior to his brother. Jeremy enjoyed making his brother feel bad about himself, and because he felt this way, he had to work extra hard to make sure he never lost to Ralphie.

Everybody wants to be recognized for being good at something. It is easy to get caught up in seeing only what others are good at and feeling jealous because we do not seem to measure up to others. This feeling becomes worse when family and friends do not recognize our own abilities and only criticize our weaknesses. People who point out the weaknesses of others are usually trying to feel better about their own shortcomings. But criticism hurts. Too much negativity may cause a person to go overboard in an attempt to prove his or her self-worth.

Internal Pressures

"Tonya, tell me something you like about yourself. Something besides the fact that you always get straight As on your report card," said Mr. Johnson. Tonya could not think of a single thing.

Mr. Johnson was Tonya's psychologist. Tonya's parents decided she should start seeing a counselor when she tried to kill herself last February. She had flunked a test, the first test she had ever failed. She was not prepared for the exam because her mother had been in the hospital for a minor operation. Tonya had been too worried about her mom to even open a book.

When she saw her grade, she almost fainted. Tonya begged her history teacher to let her retake the test, but he was very strict. So she went home and tried to slash open her wrists with a razor blade. She figured her grade point average was wrecked for good, so why bother going on living? Luckily, the razor blade was dull.

Grades were everything to Tonya. Tonya thought that she was ugly and that she didn't have any friends. She was certain that no one liked her. But since she did have a knack for getting good grades, she spent all of her time making sure that every test she took was 100 percent perfect. Now that her report card was ruined by this failed history test, she had nothing. She was nothing.

One of the most challenging internal pressures facing young people is self-esteem. Self-esteem is the feeling we have about who we are. When a person's self-esteem is low, the person does not like himself or herself. People with low self-esteem may even believe that they hate themselves, and like Tonya, may decide to try to take their own lives. Suicide is an extreme but all too common result of low self-esteem.

Suicide is an extreme but all too common result of low self-esteem.

Some parents give their children only negative messages about their looks, their abilities, or their personalities.

Where Does Low Self-Esteem Come From?

Sometimes teens are not taught how to love themselves. Maybe their parents or other people in their lives gave them only negative messages about their looks, their abilities, or their personalities. When a person is constantly told negative things about his- or herself, he or she will probably grow to believe them. This is one way in which external pressures affect internal ones.

Low self-esteem commonly leads to the need to over-achieve. Achieving is a way of disproving our worst thoughts about ourselves. It shows us that we are not worthless and that we do serve a purpose in the world. Everybody feels worthless or helpless sometimes. But those who constantly think that way often feel the need to achieve beyond reasonable boundaries. By over-achieving they hope to prove themselves worthwhile.

Sometimes low self-esteem and insecurity create a condition called "blind ambition." Some people may feel so uncertain about their place in the world that they end up hurting others. Everyone has heard the story of the star or starlet who clawed and scratched his or her way to the top. This does not happen only with famous people. Sometimes teens will betray their peers by cheating in a class election, playing dirty on the athletic field, or copying off of their classmates' papers at test time—all in an attempt to stay on top of the game. These are especially destructive ways of overachieving.

Internal and external pressures work together to create negative feelings and patterns in our lives. Some of us try to deal with those pressures through overachieving, which unfortunately creates only more problems for us. The next chapter will explore some of those problems.

Chapter Three

The Dangers of Overachieving

Overachieving for the Wrong Reasons

Jal felt as though he was on the edge of some kind of breakdown. His hands shook as he guzzled coffee to stay up late studying. When he finally decided to get a few hours of rest, he could not sleep because he was so nervous and jittery. Then he popped a sleeping pill and ended up having trouble waking up. When he could no longer rely on coffee to get him going in the morning, Jal turned to amphetamines. He told himself it was only until the school year was over, so he could maintain his A+ average and stay on the basketball, wrestling, and football teams. He also had to work part-time to pay for his gym membership.

When Jal got tired, or whenever he felt like

slacking off, all he had to do was think of what his mom had said before she left home one day and never came back. "You'll never amount to anything, Jal," she had said, shaking her head. "Your father was a loser and so are you." That was why Jal felt that he needed to do all of these things perfectly.

Taking speed seemed like the perfect solution to Jal's time crunch. With the speed, Jal would sleep only on the weekends. This way he could stay up all night during the week and get his homework done. Unfortunately, things did not work out the way he had hoped.

The more speed he took, the more difficult it became to concentrate. No matter how much he studied, the information never seemed to stay in Jal's mind. Soon his A+ average began to slip. His athletic performance was also going downhill since he could not focus. Jal became a frantic ball of uncontrolled energy. None of his goals were being accomplished, and his mind and body were ready to collapse.

Overachieving creates an unbearable level of stress in our lives. Jal's story shows some of the unpleasant and sometimes dangerous situations that stress can lead us into. Everybody has some stress in their lives, but overachievers tend to be burdened with especially high levels of stress.

Stress may also lead to mental and emotional problems, such as severe depression.

The Dangers of Too Much Stress

Stress has many symptoms that are easy to identify. Sleeping problems are a common symptom of stress. Sleep is our bodies' natural way of restoring itself, of recovering from the pain and fatigue of the day and calming our minds. Without enough sleep, we cannot face our problems with proper perspective. Stress can take away our ability to sleep normally, and lack of sleep takes away our ability to cope with stress. This can create a vicious circle that is very difficult to break out of.

Sometimes illness is a result of untreated stress. Those who are under a lot of stress may often experience headaches, nausea, back pain, dizziness, ulcers, skin breakouts, or frequent colds and flu. Our bodies' functioning is directly affected by the condition of our minds and too much stress makes it harder for us to fight off pain and disease.

Stress may also lead to mental and emotional problems, such as severe depression, anxiety, loss of memory, or anger. Even an eating disorder, such as anorexia or bulimia, can be a result of too much stress. Some people suffer from intense, stress-related anxiety attacks, where they suddenly become overwhelmed by fear, leaving them unable to function. Untreated anxiety attacks can prevent someone from leading a normal life.

Some people may actually become violent toward others or themselves when placed under a high level of stress. Or they may develop compulsive habits, such as obsessively washing their hands or repeatedly cleaning the house. In extreme cases, depression and suicide can be the tragic results of stress related to overachieving.

Drugs Are No Way to Cope

Finding ways to cope with stress is never easy. Sometimes we do things to deal with stress that only create more of the painful feelings we were trying to avoid. One of the most common unhealthy responses to stress is drug abuse. Drug abuse and stress work together in many different ways. In Jal's story, we saw how drugs became a crutch, a tool to help Jal cope with his unrealistic schedule. The drugs may have seemed like the perfect solution, but they created more stress by clouding his mind and damaging his body.

Often people use drugs with the hope of experiencing an escape from anxiety. For example, depressants such as alcohol or quaaludes may seem to give relief from nervousness. Drugs such as ecstasy, marijuana, and LSD have a reputation for offering a few hours of escape from reality. But drugs always bite back; addiction is a major risk. People using drugs to relieve stress often find that they need more and more drugs to find relief. Soon they spend more time looking for ways to get drugs than achieving their goals. A short escape can become a lifetime obsession.

Another risk of drug abuse is brain damage. Many drugs destroy important parts of the human brain. Without a correctly functioning mind, nobody can hope to deal with stress. Damaging the brain can result in mental illness, paralysis, or even death.

Drugs are very expensive. They put such a strain on the user's finances that he or she may end up stealing to support his or her habit. Many drugs are also illegal, and users risk arrest and a criminal record every time they buy a joint or pull out a vial of cocaine. It is obvious that drugs will bring only more stress to someone's life, so it is best just to stay clear of them altogether.

The Risks of Legal Drugs

Caffeine, nicotine, and herbal stimulants are legal drugs that many overachievers are tempted to abuse in order to cope with the stress in their lives. Guzzling cups of

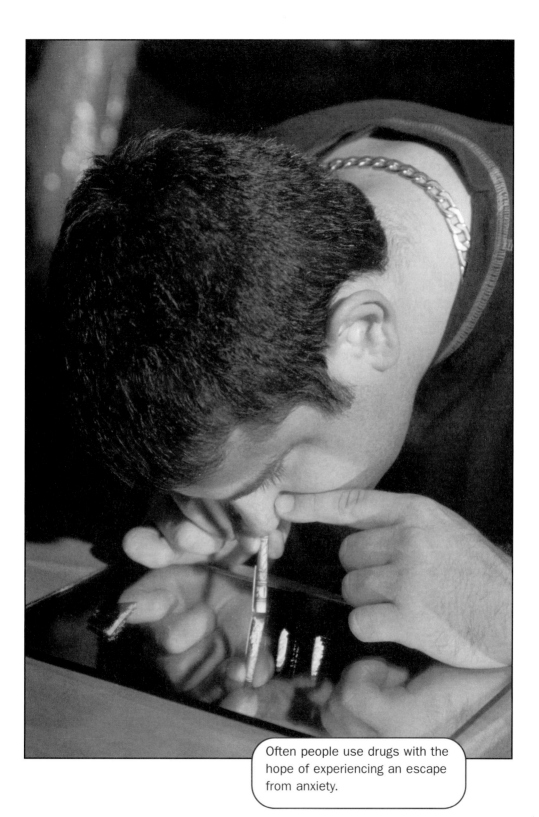

Often people use drugs with the hope of experiencing an escape from anxiety.

coffee or popping herbal uppers may seem to create energy for those late night study sessions or all-day workouts. Meanwhile, a pack-a-day cigarette habit might seem to bring a few moments of calm to an all too demanding schedule. But there are major risks associated with these drugs. In moderation, caffeine can be harmless for people who are not sensitive to the drug. But too much caffeine increases the rate of the user's heartbeat, often causing the user to feel nervous and irritable. And the more caffeine that is consumed, the more difficult it becomes to stay alert without it. When regular coffee no longer seems to do the trick, a caffeine junkie will often consume higher doses in the form of caffeine pills like Vivarin. When the caffeine wears off, fatigue and depression can set in. The same negative reaction can occur with excessive amounts of herbal stimulants like ginseng and guarana.

Smoking cigarettes is much more dangerous than using caffeine or herbal stimulants. Nicotine use creates a strong sense of dependence in the user, and quitting is extremely difficult. There are many poisonous substances in cigarette smoke besides nicotine, such as carbon monoxide and hydrogen cyanide. These gases form tar, which is a cancer causing substance. These are just a few of the risks associated with smoking. Others include back pain, lung disease, heart disease, infertility, weakened bones, premature aging, and stroke.

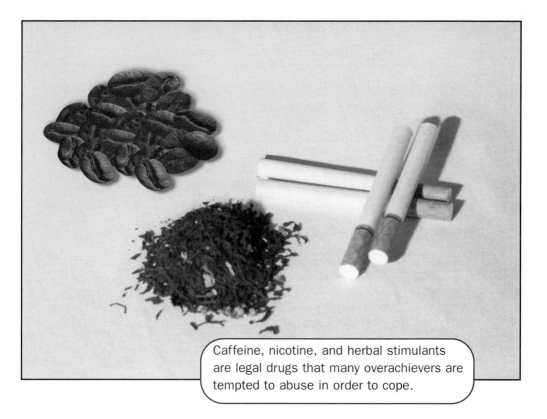

Caffeine, nicotine, and herbal stimulants are legal drugs that many overachievers are tempted to abuse in order to cope.

Overeating to Relieve Stress

Some people use food like a drug. When they start feeling stressed, they eat to find relief. This is only a temporary sense of relief and usually results in more problems. Overeating as a means of dealing with stress can cause unwanted weight gain, indigestion, heart trouble, and loss of self-esteem. It can also be an indication of a life-threatening eating disorder like bulimia nervosa or compulsive eating disorder. Some teens may end up in a cycle of obsessively dieting and working out, then bingeing to relieve their stress and feelings of low self-esteem.

Steroids

Young people who choose to overachieve in sports may turn to steroids to enhance their performance. Besides being an unfair way of winning, using steroids poses many health risks. The dangers include skin problems, weakening of the heart and blood, problems with the liver and kidneys, and muscle cramps. Some users also have seizures or convulsions, insomnia, and negative personality changes ranging from depression to violent and suicidal impulses.

There are many ineffective ways of relieving stress and enhancing your performance, but there are also many effective ways of coping with pressure. The only way to truly relieve the stress of overachieving is to learn how to work toward your goals in a reasonable way. First, however, you need to look within to understand whether you are truly an overachiever, and if so, why?

Chapter Four

How to Find Out If You Are Overachieving

Do you think of yourself as an overachiever? If so, are you worried that your drive to succeed is causing you to act or behave in ways that could be dangerous? Are you goal oriented because you want to be and because it makes you feel good, or are you trying to please someone else? It can be extremely difficult to see our own problems. It is often easier to recognize the difficulties other people are having. So if you think you might be an overachiever who is in danger of causing yourself harm, it may be helpful to go to people you trust for help. Get the opinions of friends, family, teachers, and counselors.

Here are some questions to ask yourself:

+ Do I achieve because I want to or because I feel like I have to?

If you are suffering too much stress as a result of your overachieving, ask yourself why you are pushing yourself so hard.

- Do I like myself for who I am or for what I accomplish?

- Do I drive myself beyond my limitations?

- Do I see myself as I really am or only as others see me?

- Do I allow myself to be proud of what I achieve, or do I always wish I had done better?

- Am I able to lose gracefully, or do I always need to win?

- When I make a mistake, do I learn from it and move on? Or do I beat myself up?

- Is there anyone else in my life pushing me too hard to achieve? Does he or she expect me to be perfect? Would he or she love me even if I didn't achieve?

- Do my parents' expectations of me seem reasonable or unreasonable?

- Do I view my peers as potential friends or only as competitors?

- Do I suffer from frequent fatigue, sleeplessness, anxiety, or other symptoms of unmanageable stress?

- Do I allow an adequate amount of time in my life for relaxation and recreation? When I do try to relax, do I feel guilty because I am not working on something?

- Have I ever considered drug abuse or even suicide as an escape from the pressures of my overwhelming schedule?

These questions can help you figure out if you are an overachiever who is in danger of pushing yourself too hard. Read over your answers very carefully. Think about everything you have read so far, and try to be honest with yourself.

Why Am I Overachieving?

If you think you probably are an overachiever who is suffering too much stress as a result, your next step is to ask yourself why you are pushing yourself so hard.

Psychologists and psychiatrists can be a tremendous help to young people who overachieve.

This is a difficult question to answer. Some people spend their whole lives searching for why they do the things they do. Often, a definitive answer is hard to come by. But remember, you can learn a lot if you are willing to search inside yourself for answers.

There are many trained professionals who can help you look for the answers that you seek. Psychologists and psychiatrists can be a tremendous help to young people who overachieve, both in understanding their problems and finding solutions. Some people are too afraid or embarrassed to get professional help. Many people see therapists, and it does not mean you are sick or crazy. There is no shame in letting somebody help you get to know yourself.

Dig down deep into your thoughts and feelings. How

do you really feel about who you are? What kind of childhood did you have? Were you given negative messages about yourself? Were you called weak or lazy? Did your friends or family laugh or yell at you every time you made a mistake? There are many factors that can lead to a tendency to overachieve. Just by starting to understand the feelings that lie beneath your actions, you may begin to better understand your problems and find positive ways of dealing with them. We will explore some of those ways in the next chapter.

Chapter Five

Searching for Balance

*V*iva was exhausted. She had just performed three shows in a row this week, and she had not even begun to study for her big chemistry final on Friday. It was 10:00 PM on Wednesday night, and she had just slumped down at her desk to get in an hour of cramming when her mother knocked on her door.

"Vi," called her mom. "I have wonderful news. I just got you booked for a spot on a television show for tomorrow night!" Viva nearly fainted. She decided it was time to draw the line. "I can't do it."

Sheesa just stared at her. "Can't do it?" she cried. "This could be your big break!" Viva remained firm but gentle. "Mother, I really love you. And I appreciate all you have done for me. But I just can't go on like this. I'm completely wiped out, and I have a chemistry final to study for."

Sheesa told Viva she would call her teacher to reschedule the test. "No, Mother, that's not it. I'm tired of performing. I don't want to be a star. I just want to be a teenager!" Sheesa was stunned. She had no idea that Viva felt that way. She was disappointed, but at least she finally realized what kind of pressure she was putting on her daughter. Sheesa began to wonder why she had pushed Viva so hard to be a famous singer. Because Viva said no and established boundaries, she and her mother were able to come to a new understanding.

Learn How to Say No

There are many effective ways for overachievers to work toward finding balance in their lives. One of the most important things to do is to begin to recognize the difference between reasonable and unreasonable expectations. This can be tricky, but with a little practice and experience it will become easier to find the happy and healthy medium.

Once you are able to recognize unreasonable expectations, the next step is to establish boundaries. This step requires a great deal of courage. Establishing boundaries means putting your foot down and saying no, like Viva did with her mother. It can be very liberating to stand up for yourself, and the results are worth the effort. Establishing boundaries can be a difficult and painful process, but it may be the only way to put an end to an unhealthy cycle. Ultimately a relationship becomes stronger when

It is important to recognize the difference between reasonable and unreasonable expectations, and set boundaries for yourself.

both parties communicate openly and honestly.

Unreasonable expectations come not only from others, but also from inside ourselves. You may have to establish boundaries with yourself, and say no to the negative impulses that drive you to overachieve. That can be even more difficult than saying no to others. Since you probably do not fully understand why you feel driven to overachieve, saying no to that mysterious part of yourself will be an incredible challenge. Try to come to terms with the fact that for whatever reasons, some forces within you might not be working in your best interest. And that in time—by speaking with a counselor, a therapist, another professional, or an adult whom you trust—you can reach an understanding of what those forces are, why they may work against you at times, and most important, how you can conquer them. When you can do this, you will be well on your way to learning how to turn your weaknesses into strengths.

Taking Positive Steps

Jeff was finally back home and feeling much better, after an agonizing two month stay at the hospital. What a horrible experience the whole thing had been. Jeff had been rushed to the emergency room after trying to lift a barbell at the gym that was much too heavy for him. The strain of the huge weight had made Jeff lose his balance. He slammed down on the floor of the gym, and the weight came crashing down on his left foot. During the fall, he had also suffered a severe strain in his shoulders. Even after multiple surgeries and a long hospital stay, Jeff was still not completely recovered. The surgeon told him that he was really lucky that he had not done any permanent nerve damage.

"Enough is enough," Jeff thought to himself, looking in the mirror. "This is really crazy what I am doing to myself." Jeff decided to take a good, long look at why he was driving himself so hard to become big and muscular. He looked closely at his reflection. He saw the embarrassing acne, the scars of the old zits that he had picked (even though he knew that popping and picking at zits made them worse), the big, protruding nose that

had always tormented him, and he winced at the memory of the mean things that had been said to him in the past. Jeff took a deep breath and decided that it was time to try something different.

For a change, he looked for his good qualities. In the mirror Jeff noticed that he had a well-shaped jawline and strong, blue eyes. People had always told him how great his eyes were. Also, he was in great shape. The acne was actually starting to clear up a bit, and maybe his nose was not as big as he had thought.

Then he looked even deeper. Before becoming obsessed with working out, he had been a kind, caring person. He did things for other people. He was a good listener, and everybody seemed to like him.

Jeff decided to stop being so hard on himself. Even though it was tough, when he thought about it, he knew deep down that he deserved the best.

Learning how to be positive (especially in terms of how you think of yourself) is essential to weeding out the dangerous behavior that is often a part of an overachiever's lifestyle. Remember, there is nothing wrong with reaching for the sky, having lots of ambition, and wanting to do your best. You can be an overachiever who has a positive self-image, a healthy lifestyle, and a clear sense of when to say no. What is wrong is if you are pushing yourself to succeed for the wrong reasons. A

Positive self-talk has been proven effective for people who use it correctly.

good way to get rid of the wrong reasons is by having the right attitude—a positive one.

Talking to Yourself

Some people believe that people who talk to themselves are insane. This is not always true. There are very constructive ways to talk to yourself. Just think, negative messages first came to you through spoken words. What better way to fight the effect of those messages than giving yourself new ones?

This is a method called positive self-talk, which many mental health professionals view as an important step in improving low self-esteem. It has been proven effective for people who use it correctly. Positive self-talk is very simple. All you have to do is tell yourself great things out loud, like "I am a wonderful person" or "I can do anything I set my mind to." It seems a bit silly at first, but you would be surprised at how it can change your outlook.

It can be used for anything. If you have a negative body image, say "I love my body. I have a terrific body." If you feel like you cannot do anything right, say "I am a very skillful and intelligent person. I can do anything I set my mind to."

If you are someone with a low self-image, you may not believe these things as you say them. That is okay. The whole idea is to keep saying them until eventually you really do believe them. The messages go into your subconscious, which is a part of your mind that you do not always know is there. Your subconscious controls almost everything you do, even though you do not realize it. Your subconscious understands and digests these positive messages. It then sends them out to your entire being. The more you hear the words, the more you will believe them. After all, many people say we are what we believe we are.

When and How to Practice Positive Self-Talk

When do you practice positive self-talk? ALL THE TIME. Do it when you wake up in the morning. Do it before you go to sleep at night. Do it any time you possibly can in between.

It is especially important to use self-talk to fight negative messages as they appear in your mind. Where do those negative messages come from? From your sub-conscious. You might be hard at work and feeling fine, when suddenly a voice pops into your head: "You can't do this. You're not smart enough. You'll never amount to any-thing!" These are messages you learned at some point in your life, and there is only one way to unlearn them.

So when you encounter these messages, coming from within or from somebody else, be sure to fight them with positive messages. Sometimes you cannot say them out loud. You should not interrupt your fourth period study hall to announce that you have a winning smile and stunning fashion sense. At times it may be best just to think the message silently.

It can also be helpful to write the messages down and put them in places where you know you will see them regularly. On the bathroom mirror, inside the cover of your notebook, and in your book bag are all possibili-ties. Reading the affirmations (positive messages) can be almost as effective as saying or hearing them. There are even "positive message tapes" you can buy, or you can make your own. Listening to these tapes provides fur-ther reinforcement for the subconscious.

Give Yourself Time to Relax

We all like to keep busy, but it is very important to remember that relaxation is absolutely essential for your overall health and peace of mind. An important part of beating stress and excessive pressures is setting aside

An important part of beating stress and excessive pressures is setting aside time to relax with calming activities that you enjoy.

enough time in your schedule to relax. Try to do calming activities that you enjoy. These might include reading a great novel, talking with friends, or just staring at the clouds. Many people find spiritual activities like meditation and yoga relaxing. Try not to feel guilty about the work you could be doing when relaxing. Avoiding relaxation will only hinder your progress by increasing stress.

Evaluate Your Old Habits

If there has been too much pressure on you to reach certain goals, you may have developed unhealthy habits that need to be replaced with healthy ones to beat stress. If you have been avoiding sleep in order to get more work done, try slowly to work your way back to an eight- or nine-hour-a-night sleep schedule. Sleep is an important stress reliever.

Maybe your eating habits have suffered because of your active schedule. Have you been eating junk food on the go to help keep up with your schedule or overeating to relieve stress? Maybe you have been depriving yourself of a proper diet in order to try to reach an unattainable body ideal. If you are worried that you or someone you know may have an eating disorder, do not worry—there are people you can get help from. Look at the Where to Go for Help section at the back of this book for the name of some organizations to contact. Take a good look at the way you eat, and try to work toward a sensible, balanced diet. This will help you to deal with your problems with a more positive outlook.

Have you been relying on coffee or other stimulants to give you the energy you need to keep up? Have you been using alcohol or other depressants to calm down after a busy day? If you want to achieve a balanced, healthy life, all drug use should be eliminated. The possible exception is caffeine, which should be kept to a minimum if used at all. Quitting any drugs, from cigarettes to marijuana, is a difficult process. But it is necessary to face our lives with a clear head and a stable point of view. As we read earlier, drugs always end up increasing stress in the end.

Finding the Right Balance

It may seem impossible at first, but you really can change your point of view, your habits, and your life. With a bit of effort, a good honest look at yourself, and help from others if you need it, you can begin to understand why you are overachieving in ways that are dangerous to your health. You can beat both internal and external pressure, conquer stress, and set new goals, keeping your positive self-image in mind. Reach for the sky because you want to, not because you are driven to or because you need to prove something to someone. Then you can succeed sensibly. You can build a healthy, happy future, starting today!

Glossary

affirmation A positive message you give yourself to fight negative messages and increase feelings of self-esteem.

amphetamines Illegal drugs, also known as speed, which give the user energy but have dangerous side effects.

anorexia nervosa A life-threatening eating disorder in which someone refuses to eat healthy amounts of food, if any at all.

bad pain Pain that is a signal of a serious problem: Overachievers may feel bad pain when they try to accomplish more than is humanly possible.

blind ambition A destructive way of overachieving in which someone needs to be dishonest or hurt other people to succeed.

boundaries Psychological walls we must set up between ourselves and others to prevent them from forcing unreasonable expectations upon us.

bulimia nervosa A life-threatening eating disorder in which a person habitually binges on food then purges by vomiting, using laxatives, or overexercising.

caffeine A legal drug, found in coffee and other beverages and foods, that stimulates the heart rate and can contribute to stress.

depressants Drugs that slow down the central nervous system and can have dangerous side effects.

external pressure Pressure to overachieve that comes from other people in our lives, like family and friends.

good pain Pain that tells us we are working hard, but within our limits.

healthy competition Competition between two people who respect one another and wish to help each other perform at their best.

internal pressure Pressure to overachieve that comes from within ourselves.

nicotine A legal but highly addictive drug found in cigarettes and chewing tobacco.

overachieve To achieve or accomplish beyond reasonable limitations for unhealthy reasons, such as low self-esteem or unreasonable parental expectations.

overcompensate To overachieve to make up for perceived faults or flaws in ourselves.

positive self-talk A constructive way of talking to ourselves, using positive messages or affirmations to fight negative attitudes.

self-esteem Feelings we have about ourselves.

steroids Drugs used to enhance athletic performance that can have negative consequences.

stress-related illness Physical or mental illness that results from untreated stress.

subconscious A powerful part of our minds that we do not always know is there; responds to positive self-talk, and helps us to believe affirmations.

tar A cancer-causing substance found in cigarettes.

unhealthy competition Competition between two people who do not respect one another; results in increased negative feelings and stress.

Where to Go for Help

In the United States

American Institute of Stress
124 Park Avenue
Yonkers, NY 10703
(914) 963-1200

American Self-Help Clearinghouse
http://www.cmhc.com/selfhelp

Boys Town Suicide Hotline (for boys and girls)
(800) 448-3000

Eating Disorders Awareness and Prevention (EDAP)
603 Stewart Street
Suite 803
Seattle, WA 98101
(206) 382-3587
http://members.aol.com/edapinc

Narcotics Anonymous
(818) 773-9999
http://www.netwizards.net/recovery/na/

National Mental Health Association
1021 Prince Street
Alexandria, VA 22314-2971
(800) 969-NMHA
http://www.nmha.org

Recovery Online
http://www.netwizards.net/recovery/index.html

Youth Crisis Hotline
(800) 448-4663

Also try looking in the yellow pages of your local telephone book for:
+ Counseling services for individuals and families
+ Mental health centers
+ YMCA/YWCA
+ Social service organizations
+ Psychologists

In Canada

Anorexia Nervosa and Bulimia Association (ANBA)
767 Bayridge Drive
P.O. Box 20058
Kingston, ON K7P 1C0

Canadian Mental Health Association
Barrie-Simcoe Branch
5 Bell Farm Rd.
Barrie, ON L4M 5G1
(705) 726-5033
Fax: (705) 726-0636
E-mail: cmhasim@bconnex.net

CMHA Ontario Division
80 Dundas St. W.
Suite 2301
Toronto, ON M5G 1Z8
(416) 977-5580
Fax: (416) 977-2264 or (416) 977-2813
E-mail: division@ontario.cmha.ca
Web site: www.ontario.cmha.ca

Canadian Public Health Association
1565 Carling Avenue
Suite 400
Ottawa, ON K1Z 8R1
(613) 725-3769

For Further Reading

Ayer, Eleanor H. *Everything You Need to Know About Stress.* New York: Rosen Publishing Group, 1998.

Jasheway, Leigh Anne. *Don't Get Mad, Get Funny: A Light-Hearted Approach to Stress Management.* Duluth, MN: Pfeifer-Hamilton, 1996.

Langer, Michael B. *Drugs and the Pressure to Be Perfect.* New York: Rosen Publishing Group, 1998.

Leyden-Rubenstein, Lori A. *The Stress Management Handbook.* New Canaan, CT: Keats Publishing, 1998.

Myers, Esther. *Yoga and You: Energizing and*

Relaxing Yoga for New and Experienced Students. Boston, MA: Shambhala, 1997.

Stoddard, Alexandra. *The Art of the Possible: The Path from Perfectionism to Balance and Freedom.* New York: William Morrow, 1995.

Turkington, Carol. *Stress Management for Busy People.* New York: McGraw-Hill, 1998.

Index

About the Author

John Giacobello is a freelance writer, musician, and sometimes overachiever. He lives in New York City and his first CD is coming out in the Spring of 2000.

Photo Credits

Cover and interior photos by Louis Dollagary.

Layout

Laura Murawski